THE BIOGRAPHY

OF WILL SMITH

EVERYTHING FROM WILL SMITH'S BOOK,

CHILDHOOD, LEGACY

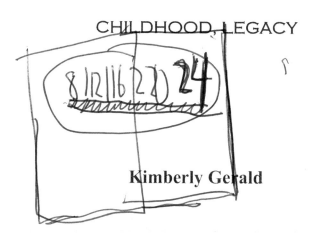

Kimberly Gerald

TABLE OF CONTENTS

EARLY LIFE

Willard Christopher Smith Jr. was born the second of four children to Willard Smith Sr and Caroline Smith on September 25 1968. As the second child, he had an elder sister Pamela born in 1964, and two younger siblings (twins), Harry and Ellen, born in 1971. Both parents were very influential in their children's childhood. Willard Sr. belonged to the US Air Force until he decided to start up his own enterprise, which was a refrigeration business. Willard Sr. was both the owner and engineer of his new enterprise capable of installing long freezer cases, which are popularly found in supermarkets, as well as owning an ice company tasking with suppling large blocks for supermarket use. Caroline being a graduate of Carnegie Mellon, was a school administrator in the School District of Philadelphia. A firm adherent of ever learning, which she dutifully passed onto her children. It was known that correct grammar usage in her house was a must and she did not like hearing slang. Smith credits his ever-burning desire to learn to his mom, his strong work ethic to his Father, and his philanthropy to his Grandmother, whom he believed to be the kindest soul.

The Smiths were Baptist, and irrespective of their denomination, attended a primarily white Catholic school. The Smith family lived in Wynnefield; a middle-class area predominantly African American. Will, at 12, began rapping at parties with his friends; rap was something he had a flair for, and his love for Eddie Murphy and Grandmaster would be a key influence in his future. Though Will lacked his mother's enthusiasm for academics, he was nevertheless a bright student. He attended the prestigious Julia Reynolds Masterman Laboratory and Demonstration School, which is a high-tier secondary for select individuals who possess high academic proficiency. Due to a lack of interest in Academia as an A student, he would often get B graded results for his lack of commitment. When Will was 13, his parents divorced, and though they were separated, they all lived in the same neighborhood. For high school, Will attended the famous Philadelphia's Overbrook High School, a school which boasts of highly accomplished alumni whose individuals include film producer James Lassiter, basketball stars Malik Rose and Wayne Hightower, sports radio icon Phillip Allen, astronaut Guion S. Bluford Jr., Negro League baseball legend Bill Cash, and Wilt Chamberlain, one of the greatest NBA players of all Time.

CAREER

In Overbrook, Will met Jeff Townes, who was quite popular as a DJ in school, they became fast friends. The two decided to collaborate on music and created their unique personal style, which comprised scratching records, cuss-free lyrics, and incorporating comedy. After SAT, there was the choice of applying to the Massachusetts Institute of Technology (MIT), which he didn't think twice about not following. Following his love for music, he and Townes began writing and rehearsing and eventually performed in the Battle of the Bands at the 1986 New Music Seminar. Townes won the DJ competition, and this gave them a bit of renown and soon after signed a recording contract with Jive Records. In 1987 while Smith was still in school, the duo released their debut album Rock the House. The ten raps on the Album were "Don't Even Try It," "Girls Ain't Nothing but Trouble," "Guys Ain't Nothing but Trouble," "Just One of Those Days," "Just Rockin'," "The Magnificent

Jazzy Jeff," "Rock the House," "Special Announcement," "Takin' It to the Top," and "Touch of Jazz." Smith wrote most of the rhymes in their collaborations, while Townes was innovative with the scratching and mixing. DJ Jazzy Jeff and the Fresh Prince's debut single, "Girls Ain't Nothing but Trouble," from the debut album, was developed based on the theme song from the popular 1960s television sitcom I Dream of Jeannie. The success of both the single and Rock the House gave him much in popularity and wealth.

In 1988 the duo of Fresh Prince and DJ Jazzy Jeff released their second Album, He's the DJ, I'm the Rapper, which comprised various radio hits "Parents Just Don't Understand," "Brand New Funk," and "Nightmare on My Street." In 1989, the duo won the Favorite Rap Artist and Favorite Rap Album at the American Music Awards ceremony in Los Angeles. Will Smith and Jeff Townes would bag the first-ever Grammy to be given to a rap artist for the Album He's the DJ, I'm the Rapper. It became the first-ever hip-hop album to reach double platinum 1989 also saw the duo make another hit record, "And In This Corner," their third Album released in October. It reached #39 on the U.S Billboard 200 albums chart. It comprised 12 songs, "Then she bit me," "I think I can beat Mike Tyson," "Jazzy's Groove," "Everything That Glitters (Ain't Always Gold)," "You Got it (Donut)," "The Girlie had a Moustache," "The Reverend," "Who Stole my Car," "The Men of Your Dreams," "Numero Uno," "Too Damn Hype" and "Jeff Waz on the Beat Box." The Album won no awards but received two Grammy Awards nominations

Benny Medina began the development of the soon-to-be Fresh Prince of Bel-Air, which incorporated Will's rapper name into the title. The show started airing on NBC from September 10 1990 to May 20 1996, lasting six seasons and spanning 148 episodes. It centered on Will Smith as a street exposed teen born and raised in West Philadelphia whose mom sends him to live with his wealthy uncle and aunt in their Bel- Air mansion. While living with them, his values and lifestyle often clash with his more financially comfortable relatives. The show received many nominations and won awards like the Top TV for the ASCAP Film and Television Music Awards, TP de Oro in the Best Foreign Series (Mejor Serie Extranjera), etc.

While star acting for the Fresh Prince of Bel-Air, he and DJ Jazzy Jeff continued making music. On July 23, 1991, the two released Homebase, with "Summertime" and "Ring My Bell." Smith and Townes would later win a Grammy Award for "Summertime," centered on the summers growing up in Philadelphia. The Album reached the number 5 on the Top R&B/Hip-Hop albums Charts and attained number 12 on the Billboards 200. The Album included "I'm all that," "Summertime," "The Things That U Do," "This Boy is Smooth," "Ring My Bell," "A Dog is a Dog," "Caught in the Middle (Love& Life," "Trapped on the Dance Floor," "Who

Stole the DJ," "You Saw My Blinker," "dumb Dancin," "Summertime (Reprise)." The Album became certified Platinum and also won an American Music Award for Favorite Rap/ Hip-Hop Album in 1992

On October 12, 1993, the duo released their fifth and final studio album Code Red, which did not break as many records as their previous albums. The Album reached number 64 on the Billboard 200 and 39 on the Top R&B/ Hip-Hop Albums. In early 1994 the Album was later certified Gold by the Recording Industry Association of America. "Boom! Shake the Room", "I'm Looking for the One (To Be with Me)," "I Wanna Rock," and Can't-Wait to be with You" were four tracks of the Album which attained a spot on billboard100. Other ways include; "Somethin' Like Dis," "Twinkle Twinkle (I'm Not a Star), "Code Red," "Shadow Dreams," "Just Kickin' It," "Ain't No Place Like Home," "Scream," "Boom! Shake the Room" (street Remix)

Will Smith decided to focus on acting and hence the unofficial split with his friend DJ Jazzy Jeff. In 1992 Smith bagged his first movie role in Where the Day Takes You, directed by Marc Rocco. It centered on a group of homeless teens trying to survive on the hardened streets of Los Angeles. A year later, in 1993, Smith landed another small part in Made in America, directed by Richard Benjamin starring Whoopi Goldberg and Ted Danson. In 1993, Smith landed a role in the film adaptation of the hit plays Six Degrees of Separation, directed by Australian Fred Schepisi. Co-starring in the film with Smith were Donald Sutherland and Stockard Channing. The story centered on a hustler (Smith's character) who cons his way into the Manhattan apartment of a wealthy couple (Channing's and Sutherland's characters) by convincing them he is the son of noted actor Sidney Poitier and their son's friend from school. Summer of 1995 saw Director Michael Bay's Bad Boys in the theaters. This top-tier-budget cop movie starred Smith (as

Detective Mike Lowery) and Martin Lawrence (as Detective Marcus Burnett)—both black actors who came from a background of sitcoms—Smith from The Fresh Prince Bel-Air and Lawrence from Martin. The movie did not get high praise from Critics, though many reviewers lauded Smith's and Lawrence's acting abilities. The film earned them a nomination for the MTV Movie Awards Best On-Screen Duo award.

1996 saw the release of the much-acclaimed Independence Day, which was undoubtedly one of the hottest summer blockbusters of the year. The movie was directed by Roland Emmerich, who co-wrote the screenplay along with Dean Delvin. It was Smith's first box-office smash hit and put to rest all doubts on his ability as a capable actor. In its opening weekend in the United States alone, the movie brought in over $50 million. In 1997 Men in Black was released on the big screens, another considerable elevation in Smith's Career. Here, Smith saved the world and fought aliens as Secret Agent J (James Darrel Edwards III). Ed

Solomon wrote the screenplay, and Barry Sonnenfeld directed it. The movie also starred Tommy Lee Jones (secret Agent K), partnering with Agent J to stop the aliens' apocalyptic plans for the earth. Smith wrote two of the songs on the Men in Black Soundtrack. The Album, including the theme song, "Men in Black," was Smith's first solo record, Big Willie Style. Another hit song on Big Willie Style was "Just the Two of Us." Big Willie Style went on to become multiplatinum. The hit single "Getting' Jiggy Wit It" gave Smith the first No. 1 single solo career. The success of Independence Day and Men in Black—both with their huge US opening weekend sales led Smith to term his weekend-opening blockbusters as a "Big Willie Weekend."

Smith and his manager Lassiter soon began their own Production Company, Overbrook Entertainment which went on to produce numerous movies and plays and even music; plays (Jitney); films (Ali, Showtime, Saving Face, Hitch, ATL, The Pursuit of Happyness, I Am Legend, Hancock, Lakeview

Terrace, The Secret Life of Bees, Seven Pounds, and I, Robot); television (All of Us); and music (The Evolution of Robin Thicke, Wicked Wisdom). Initially, Overbrook Entertainment collaborated with Universal Pictures to make movies, but after three years of nothing, they switched partnerships to Sony. In 1998, Enemy of State was Smith's next big project where he co-starred Gene Hackman. Tony Scott directed, and David Marconi wrote the screenplay. Smith had long admired Hackman and was thrilled to work with him. The movie earned Smith an NAACP Image Award nomination for Outstanding Actor in a Motion Picture. In its opening weekend in the United States, Enemy of State made more than $20million.

1999 was not a good year as Will made some bad career choices, first was his turning down the lead part of Neo in The Matrix, the science fiction that would later receive massive accolades. However, he took part in the sci-fi cowboy film Wild Wild West, based on a favorite childhood television series from 1965 to 1969. Though the film was unsuccessful, Smith's original musical track was a hit (Willenium). Overall, reviewers had no good thing to say about the movie as James Berardinelli wrote, "[Wild Wild West] lacks energy and the characters display little charisma." The San Francisco Chronicle affirmed Sonnenfeld "can't seem to get anything going here."

In 2000 The Legend of Bagger Vance helped Smith to regain his momentum. The movie is based on a novel by Steven Pressfield (Jeremy Leven wrote the screenplay) in which a struggling golfer attempts to recover both his game and his life with help from his mystical caddy. In 2001, Smith released a children's book based on his 1997 song "Just the Two of Us." Published by Scholastic Books, the text of the 32-page book, also called Just the Two of Us, is composed of Smith's lyrics illustrated with Kadir Nelson's expressive drawings. This publication would put Smith in the light as a published author. In 2001, Michael Mann, the prodigious director of Heat (1995) and the Insider (1999), was pushing to bring a movie on the famous world heavyweight boxer Muhammed Ali to the theaters. Ali appeared on the big screens in December 2001 and was the decisive push Smith needed in his career. Mann and Smith's hard work paid off, and Ali got Smith an Oscar nomination for the best actor at the Academy Awards. Men in Black II (2002) and Bad Boys II (2003) were not as great as their prequels.

Will and Jada Smith co-created their television sitcom for UPN, All of Us, which premiered in 2003. Which was centered on a blended family (with biological and stepparents) similar to the Smiths', starred Duane Martin and Lisa Raye. The Smiths' son, Jaden, had a recurring role as Reggie. When the sitcom finished its third season, UPN merged with The WB to birth The CW network. The new network picked up All of Us, which received the sought-after time slot behind the hit series Everybody Hates Chris. During its four-year run, it nominated all of us for an

NAACP Image Award in the Outstanding Comedy Series category in 2007

In 2004, Smith served the role of Detective Del Spooner in the live adaptation of Isaac Asimov's sci-fi classic, I, Robot, directed by Alex Proyas. Smith's character is a detective investigating a murder in the year 2035. The film also stars Chi McBride, Bridget Moynahan, Bruce Greenwood, James Cromwell, and Alan Tudyk. The film got an Oscar nominee for Best Achievement in Visual Effects at the Academy Awards in 2005. It made more than $52 million in its opening weekend. In 2004, Smith took on his first animated film when he voiced Oscar in Shark Tale's famous children's movie. Providing voices were co-stars Robert De Niro, Renée Zellweger, Jack Black, and Angelina Jolie. In its opening week, the film earned more than $47million. Along with his production company Overbrook Entertainment and Sony, Will Smith bought John Keller's story, nicknamed the Can man, for his heroic efforts in rescuing 244 of his neighbors during Hurricane Katrina.

In 2005, Smith landed the lead role as Alex Hitchens in the romantic comedy movie Hitch. He also wrote and performed the theme song, which he would later include in his Album, Lost and Found, released that same year. Kevin Bisch wrote the screenplay, and Eva Mendes directed the film. With Hitch's premiere in Europe, Smith bagged a spot in the Guinness Book of World Records as the actor to have made the most public appearances in 12 hours on February 22, 2005. That day, he walked the red carpet three times to introduce the premieres of Hitch in England at Manchester, Birmingham, and later London all in half a day. This title he would later lose to German actors Jürgen Vogel and Daniel Brühl, who attended four red-carpet premieres for their movie, Ein Freund von mir, in October 2006. In 2006, Smith offered to work on The Pursuit of Happyness, which he gladly accepted. The film, which Gabriele

Muccino directed, was a winner but received mixed reviews. His son Jaden starred as Smith's son in the movie, and their synergy on set was incredible. Though many reviewed the film as unexceptional, the Father and son performance was termed excellent, which got Smith a nomination for an Academy Award for Best Actor.

I Am Legend which appeared in theaters as of 2007, was a remake of the 1971 film Omega Man which starred Charlton Heston as Robert Neville as the last man on earth in the movie, which was also a remake of The Last Man on Earth (1964) which starred Vincent Price. Francis Lawrence and Mark Rotosevich directed the film in 2007, and Akiva Goldsman developed the screenplay. Irrespective of the film being a remake, it was a worldwide hit netting $77 million in its opening weekend in the United States. Hancock, Smith's next film, was directed by Peter Berg and written by Vince Gilligan and Vincent Ngo. Overbrook Entertainment was responsible for producing the film, and co-starring with him were Charlize Theron, Jason Bateman, and Jae Head. Smith had the lead spot of Hancock, a superhero who hated the fact he was a superhero and an appalling drunk. Hancock had mixed reviews but could still net over $62 million in its opening weekend, mainly due to Smith's fame. In 2008, Smith produced and starred in the movie Seven Pounds, which Grant Nieporte directed by Gabriele Muccino. Later on, Smith would make several movies in which he would have no starring role. Through Overbrook Entertainment, Smith would help produce Lakeview Terrace, The Human Contract, and The Secret Life of Bees in 2008 and The Karate Kid in 2010.

August 19, 2011, saw the world receiving the announcement of Smith returning to the studio to work on his fifth studio album. He ended his role as Agent J in the sequel Men in Black III (2012), after which he decided he would be with the MIB franchise. In 2013 he starred in After Earth with his son Jaden and the movie was disappointing and termed "the most painful failure of Will Smith's career." which gave him an almost two-year break from acting. In 2015 he co-starred with Margot Robbie in Focus, which was released in late February of 2015. His next movie was Concussion, where Smith played the role of Dr. Bennet Omalu of the Brain Injury Research Institute, being the first to discover chronic traumatic encephalopathy. In 2016, Smith took on the part of Deadshot in DC's Suicide Squad, which he chose over a role in Independence Day: Resurgence. That same year he featured in Collateral Beauty, directed by David Frankel. Smith's Bright urban fantasy movie, which was distributed by Netflix three days to Christmas in 2017, remains Netflix's most expensive film to date. He also released the song "Get Lit" in collaboration with Jazzy Jeff that same year.

Smith portrayed The Genie in Disney's 2019 live adaptation of Aladdin and was instrumental in producing some singles in the movie's soundtracks: "Arabian Nights (2019)", "Friend Like

Me" and "Prince Ali." Aladdin would later gross over a billion dollars making it Will Smith's highest-grossing movie. Smith played a lead role in Ang Lee's Gemini Man (2019), where he had to battle it out with a younger cloned version of himself. Later in 2019, he co-starred with Tom Holland in an animated film Spies in Disguise, released on Christmas of 2019. In 2020 he and Martin Lawrence executed a third film for the Bad Boys franchise called the Bad Boys for Life which received good critical acclaim and varying nominations in the BET Awards, Critic's Choice Super Awards, People's Choice Awards, and the Saturn Awards. Its box office earnings were reported to be at $426.5 million even with the COVID restrictions.

PERSONAL LIFE

He was only 18 years old when he became a millionaire largely due to the success of "Girls ain't Nothing "and "Rock the House". But his financial success was rather abrupt as he squandered his wealth on family and friends. On May 9, 1992, Smith got married to Sheree Zampino Fletcher, and they had a child Willard III who was also called Trey. The marriage lasted only three years as both partners could not cope with Will's consuming career. They had met at a taping of the television sitcom A Different World back in 1991. On 1997, December 31, Will married Jada Pinkett, whom he had met years earlier, and had two children, Jaden, born on July 8, 1998, and Willow, who had October 31, 2000. The marriage thrives till today, even after experiencing several obstacles. Will and Jada's home schooled their children as they believed in a more hands-on education for their kids.

In April 2013, some comments from Jada made people question if she was in an open marriage. Rumors would later surface that the couple was on the verge of divorce. In 2005, Will had to silence the wagging tongue by writing on his Facebook: "In the interest of redundant, repetitious, over and over again-ness... Jada and I are... NOT GETTING DIVORCE!!!!!!!!". This Jada reinforced in her 2018 interview on Sway in the Morning.

In 2016 Willard Smith Sr. died of cancer. In recent years much details of Will and Jada's marriage have come to light as during one of Jada's Red table sessions where both of them appeared and Jada talked about an affair she had with R&B singer August Alsina in 2016. During Jada and Will's separation, she got into an 'entanglement" with August Alsina in a way to help him as the R&B singer was purported to be sick and dealing with several issues, one of which was an addiction. During this Time Smith was rumored to be in a relationship with Heidy De La Rosa. Every year, Smith takes his mother, Caroline, to the

Canyon Ranch Spa in Tucson, Arizona, for a vacation. Currently, Caroline wears a prosthetic leg after breaking her left leg and requiring amputation after suffering from a nasty infection, and she spends much of her Time helping others.

POLITICS, RELIGION, AND CHARITY

Politically, Will Smith is what one would term as a Liberal Democrat and has not shied away from making his political stand known. January of 1993 saw Smi9th host the Presidential Inaugural Celebration for Youth as part of President Bill Clinton's gala. In 2008, Smith supported Senator Barack Obama of Illinois with donations to his presidential campaign on the Democratic ticket. The Smith Family hosted the Nobel Peace Prize Concert at Oslo Spektrum in Oslo, Norway, on December 11, 2009, which honored the former President of the United States of America, President Barack Obama, with the 2009 Nobel Peace Prize. Smith's views on religion are open-minded, curious, and very much personal as he does not believe in any organized religion.

In 2004 the Smiths donated $20,000 to the Hollywood Education and Literacy Program (HELP), which serves as a foundation for Scientology's homeschooling. (Scientology is the study of truth and the "handling of the spirit concerning itself, others, and all of life founded by Ron Hubbard.) in 2008 the Smith's couple funded the New Village Leadership Academy, a private elementary school in Calabasas, California. A school dedicated to Scientology focuses primarily on how-to-study methodologies, including Study Technology, developed by Hubbard.

The Smith Family established the Will and Jada Family Foundation, which aimed to improve youth education, inner-city neighborhood and community development, and lower-class families and children. In 2006 the foundation donated $1 million to the high school from which Pinkett Smith graduated, the Baltimore School for the Arts. She requested that a theater at the school be established in honor of Tupac Shakur's. In

2007, the Lupus Foundation of America (LFA) and Maybelline, in cooperation with the Will and Jada Smith Family Foundation, hosted the first Butterflies Over Hollywood benefit held in the El Rey Theatre in Los Angeles. In 2008 the Smiths donated more than $1.3 million to various religious, civic, and arts groups through the Will and Jada Smith Family Foundation. In early2010, the couple declared they would be raising funds for the United Nations World Food Programme (WFP). These funds were to help alleviate the suffering of the displaced indigenes of Haiti. They lost so much in the aftermath of the 7.0 magnitude earthquake, which struck the island nation and devastated the capital of Port-au-Prince on January 12, 2010.

AWARDS

Below are a few samples of the awards Will Smith has won over the years:

2019   Choice Sci-Fi/Fantasy Movie Actor in Aladdin

2016   MTV Generation Award for Himself

2015   Hollywood Film Awards, actor Award for Concussion

2009   BET Awards, Favorite Actor

NAACP Image Awards, Outstanding Actor in a Motion Picture for Seven Pounds

2008   Saturn Awards, Best Actor for I Am Legend

Choice Movie Actor: Horror/Thriller for I Am Legend

MTV Awards, Best Male Performance for I am Legend

2007 Jackie Coogan Award- Contribution to Youth through Motion Pictures for The Pursuit of Happyness

Choice Movie Actor: Drama for The Pursuit of Happyness

Choice Movie: Chemistry (with Jaden Smith) for The Pursuit of Happyness

2005 Choice Movie Actor: Comedy for Hitch

2002 BET Awards, Favorite Actor

2000 ASCAP Awards, Most Performed Songs for Wild Wild West

1999 Image Awards, Entertainer of the Year

ShoWest Awards, Actor of the Year

Blockbuster Awards, Favorite Actor for Enemy of the State

1998 Blockbuster Awards, Favorite Actor for Men in Black

ASCAP Awards, Most Performed Songs for Men in Black

MTV Movie Awards, Best Fight for Men in Black

MTV Movie Awards, Best Song for Men in Black

1997 Grammy Awards, Best Rap Solo Performance for Men in Black

MTV Movie Awards, Best Kiss for Independence Day

Blockbuster Awards, Favorite Actor for Independence Day

ShoWest Convention, International Box Office Achievement

1995   ShoWest Convention, Male Star of Tomorrow

1991   Grammy Awards, Best Rap Duo Performance for "Summertime."

1988   Grammy Awards, Best Rap Performance for "Parents Just Don't Understand."

NOMINATIONS

2019   Saturn Awards, Best Supporting Actor for Aladdin

2016   Choice Movie Actor: AnTEENcipated for Suicide Squad

NAACP Image Awards, Outstanding Actor in a Motion Picture for Concussion

2012   Choice Summer Movie Star: Male for Men in Black III

Choice Movie Chemistry (with Josh Brolin) for Men in Black III

2009   Saturn Awards, Best Actor for Hancock

2007   Academy Awards, Best Actor for The Pursuit of Happyness

2004   NAACP Image Awards, Outstanding Actor in a Motion Picture for Bad Boys II

2003   Best Performance by An Actor in an Effects Film for Men in Black II

2002   Academy Awards, Best Actor for Ali

Golden Globe Awards, Best Actor for Ali

2001   Saturn Awards, Best Supporting Actor for The Legend of Bagger Vance

2000   Blockbuster Awards, Favorite Action Team for Wild Wild West

Blockbuster Awards, Favorite Song for Wild Wild West

1999   Image Awards, Outstanding Lead Actor for Enemy of the State

MTV Movie Awards, Best Performance for Enemy of the State

1998   MTV Movie Awards, Best Comedic Performance for Men in Black

MTV Movie Awards, Best On-Screen Duo for Men in Black

1997   Image Awards, Outstanding Lead Actor for Fresh Prince of Bel-Air

MTV Movie Awards, Best Performance for Independence Day

1996   Image Awards, Outstanding Lead Actor for Fresh Prince of Bel-Air

MTV Movie Awards, Best On-Screen Duo for Bad Boys

1994   Golden Globe Awards, Best Actor for Fresh Prince of Bel-Air

1993   Golden Globe Awards, Best Actor for Fresh Prince

of Bel-Air

ACHIEVEMENTS

Will Smith has already left an indelible mark on the entertainment world. In 2004, 2005, and 2006, will Smith was listed as one of the 50 Most Powerful People in Hollywood. In 2005, premiere ranked will smith a number 44 on the Greatest Movie Stars of All Time for its "Stars in Our Constellation" feature. In 2006, Time listed will Smith as one of the 100 Most Influential People. In 2007, Entertainment Weekly named will Smith, one of the Top 25 Entertainers of the Year. In 2007 and 2008, Forbes.com named Smith among the 100 Most Powerful Celebrities. And his popularity has garnered high financial rewards: In 2004, his net worth was estimated to be $188 million; in 2007, Forbes estimated his earnings for the year at $31 million. In 2013, Forbes credited Smith as being the most bankable star in the world. Currently, the only actor to have starred in eight consecutive films grossed over a 100million dollars in the United States, eleven straight movies to have passed the$150 million benchmark internationally, and eight successive movies to have attained the number one in the US box office at their opening. As of 2021, Will Smith's net worth estimating to be at $350 million with four Grammy Awards, two Academy Awards, and nominations for five Golden Globe Awards, and he is still thirsty for more.

80058875R00031